Dr Myles Munroe said: "Don't let your dreams die with you"

To the Holy Spirit I give thanks for inspiring me to write this book.

Is Heaven Truly Promised unto You?

John J. Christ Noble

Is Heaven Truly Promised unto You?

Contents

Dedications

To my late father, Julius Noble who always believed in me, speaking prosperity over my life. My mother, Magda Noble who prays for me daily, believes in me and my success despite the difficult upbringing.

My wife Jackie, my children Rochelle, Jonique, Mckayla and grandson Marcus for their continued love and support. Rise Up In Faith Ministries. Annaline Clarke for the assistance in the translation of this book.

To everyone celebrating my life and my sucesses.

Introduction:

The intention of this book is not to influence your decisions.

Ask the Holy Spirit for guidance when you examine the scriptures regardless of your previous thinking.

People got so attached to the concepts of heaven and their encounter with the Creator of heaven and earth that they just wanted to be there. This was their goal. In their seeking after going to heaven, it became more about the house than the Owner of the house. Many people see themselves with their families and their pets in heaven, to get away from the things of this temporary world. They fantasize about their daily walk with God and the streets paved with gold; no more tears and reuniting with their loved ones. The questions remain: Was this the ultimate plan of God? Is this what John 14v2 all about?

Chapter 1: In the beginning

Gen 1v26 *"And God said, Let us make man in our image, after our likeness: and let them have dominion over the fish of the sea and over the fowl of the air, and over the cattle, and over all the earth, and over every creeping thing that creepeth upon the earth."*

The council's decision was final. The naming of all earthly things was the decision given to Adam and as he named everything, so it was.

Amos 3v7 *"Surely the Lord God will do nothing, but he revealed his secret unto his servants the prophets."*
He tells us everything beforehand …

Gen 18v17 *"And the Lord said, Shall I hide from Abraham that thing which I do."*
Everything was revealed to Adam as it was to Abraham. Abraham looked forward to the city with foundations.

Heb 11v10 *"For he looked for a city which hath foundations, whose builder and maker is God."* **Heb 11v16** *"But now they desire a better country, that is, an heavenly: wherefore God is not ashamed to be called their God: for he hath prepared them a city."*

Adam and Eve were removed from the garden, but only so that redemption could take place.

Gen 3v22 *"And the Lord God said, Behold, the man is become as one of us, to know good and evil: and now, lest he put forth his hand, and take also of the tree of life, and eat, and live forever."* **Gen 3v23** *"Therefore the Lord God sent him forth in the garden of Eden, to till the ground from whence he was taken."*

If He had not expelled them, God's plan would have never worked to send us a redeemer. The plan of God was always to bring us back to the garden.

Psalm 92v13 *"Those that be planted in the house of the Lord shall flourish in the courts of our God."*
Paul saw this mystery and the scripture teaches us.

1 Peter 1v12 *"Unto whom it was revealed, that not unto themselves, but unto us they did minister the things, which are now reported unto you by them that have preached the gospel unto you with the Holy Ghost sent down from heaven; which things the angels desire to look into."*

The angels were excited to see what was going to happen. Beloved, we always triumph in Christ Jesus.

2 Cor 2v14 *"Now thanks be unto God, which always caused us to triumph in Christ, and maketh manifest the savour of his knowledge by us in every place."*

It is funny how the "going to heaven" option states that people will go and live in "mansions" with their own families.

Matt 22v29 *"But Jesus replied to them, 'You are all wrong because you know neither the Scriptures [which teach the resurrection] nor the power of God [for He is able to raise the dead]'."* **Matt 22v30** *"For in the resurrection neither do men marry nor are women given in marriage, but they are like angels in heaven [who do not marry nor produce children]."* **Matt 22v31** *"But as to the resurrection of the dead--have you not read [in the Scripture] what God said to you:"* **Matt 22v32** *"'I am the God of Abraham, and the God of Isaac, and the God of Jacob'? He is not the God of the dead, but of the living."* **Matt 22v33** *"When the crowds heard this, they were astonished at His teaching."*

Scripture says that we are born from God whereby Christ is the cornerstone; we are the body where Christ is the Head. The Word of the Lord, Creator of heaven and earth and all that is in it; is to some a wonderful story of encouragement; to some it is the weapon to cage others and to strip them of their material belongings; whilst to others it is just the unchangeable plan, vision and mission of Abba Father with humanity.

The scripture teaches us in **Hosea 4v6** *"My people are destroyed for lack of knowledge: because thou hast rejected knowledge, I will also reject thee, that thou shalt be no priest to me: seeing thou hast forgotten the law of thy God, I will also forget thy children."*

What I find most disturbing is that churches of the Christian faith are such "copy and paste" ministries and this proves that the power of the Word is absent. We are becoming more and more theological about the Word then being led by the Holy Spirit. The Bible teaches us that we, who are led by the Spirit, are called children of God.

Deut 29v29 *"The secret things belong unto the LORD our God: but those things which are revealed belong unto us and to our children for ever, that we may do all the words of this law."*

At this point I am suggesting that you take time to investigate the scriptures and distinguish between them.

Jesus says in **Matt 24v14** *"And this gospel of the kingdom shall be preached in the entire world for a witness unto all nations; and then shall the end come."* The question is: Is the church teaching a religious or a kingdom gospel?

At a funeral the preacher says in **John 14v2** *"In my Father's house are many mansions: if it were not so, I would have told you. I go to prepare a place for you."*

He goes on to say that Jesus is still busy preparing the place and as soon as He is finished, He will come for us and we will be with Him forever. I could not understand the fact that Jesus is still going to prepare a place, and here we have hell on earth?

Earth is the eternal home for people. God cannot give up on His original plan with people by taking us to Heaven, as it's never been promised to people. Due to our disobedience, we lost our position. Because a person, Adam, gave up our position; our Father had to come to earth in the form of a man to reposition us. Christ was tempted in the wilderness by the devil.

Luke 4v5 *"And the devil, taking him up into a high mountain, showed unto him all the kingdoms of the world in a moment of time."* **Luke 4v6** *"And the devil said unto him, all this power will I give thee, and the glory of them: for that is delivered unto me; and to whomsoever I will I give it."*

He was talking about our authority we had over him and Eve gave it away in the garden of Eden. Christ came to strip the devil from this power and He handed authority back to us. **Psalm 24v1** *"A Psalm of David. The earth is the LORD'S, and the fullness thereof; the world, and they that dwell therein."*

The devil had rulership over a worldly system, not of the earth. When He said: "It is Finished," everything changed.

Col 2v1 *"Blotting out the handwriting of ordinances that were against us, which was contrary to us, and took it out of the way, nailing it to His cross."*
Col 2v15 *"And having spoiled principalities and powers, he made a show of them openly, triumphing over them that were in it."* **Col 2v13 [NIV]** *"When you were dead in your sins and in the uncircumcision of your flesh, God made you alive with Christ. He forgave us all our sins,* **Col 2v14** *"having cancelled the charge of our legal indebtedness, which stood against us and condemned us; he has taken it away, nailing it to the cross."* **Col 2v15** *"And having disarmed the powers and authorities, he made a public spectacle of them, triumphing over them by the cross."*

Many people just hang onto the Scripture as "proof" of going to heaven.

John 14v1 *"Let not your heart be troubled: ye believe in God, believe also in me."* **John 14v2** *"In my Father's house are many mansions: if it were not so, I would have told you. I go to prepare a place for you."* **John 14v3** *"And if I go and prepare a place for you, I will come again, and receive you unto myself; that where I am, there ye may be also."*
Beloved, you must get the revelation that you were not created for Heaven, but to live on earth. What Jesus meant when He said He is going to the cross, *He meant that He*

would restore the position that we had lost. He mentions this before His crucifixion, because the word teaches us that our sin separated us from the glory of God. Our sin removed us from our position.

Isaiah 59v2 *"But your iniquities have separated between you and your God, and your sins have hid his face from you that he will not hear."*

The cross was Abba Father's plan to bring us back into the Holy Family. Look at this passage of scripture ... **John 20v6** *"Then cometh Simon Peter following him, and went into the sepulchre, and seeth the linen clothes lie,"* **John 20v7** *"And the napkin, that was about his head, not lying with the linen clothes, but wrapped together in a place by itself."* **John 20v8** *"Then went in also that other disciple, which came first to the sepulchre, and he saw, and believed."* **John 20v9** *"For as yet they knew not the scripture, that he must rise again from the dead."* **John 20v10** *"Then the disciples went away again unto their own home."* **John 20v11** *"But Mary stood without at the sepulchre weeping: and as she wept, she stooped down, and looked into the sepulchre,"* **John 20v12** *"And seeth two angels in white sitting, the one at the head, and the other at the feet, where the body of Jesus had lain."* **John 20v13** *"And they say unto her, Woman, why weepest thou? She saith unto them, Because they have taken away my Lord, and I know not where they have laid him."* **John 20v14** *"And when she had thus said, she turned herself back, and saw Jesus standing, and knew not that it was Jesus."* **John**

20v15 *"Jesus saith unto her, Woman, why weepest thou? whom seekest thou? She, supposing him to be the gardener, saith unto him, Sir, if thou have borne him hence, tell me where thou hast laid him, and I will take him away."* **John 20v16** *"Jesus saith unto her, 'Mary'. She turned herself, and saith unto him, Rabboni; which is to say, Master."* **John 20v17** *"Jesus saith unto her, Touch me not; for I am not yet ascended to my Father: but go to my brethren, and say unto them, I ascend unto my Father, and your Father; and to my God, and your God."* **John 20v18** *"Mary Magdalene came and told the disciples that she had seen the Lord, and that he had spoken these things unto her. Wow! He said brethren, family. my Father and your Father life is in His Blood we are forgiven; set free, adopted into His Family."*

To receive any promise from Abba Father we need to be in a position to receive and that position is in His Son.

Col 2v13 *"And you, being dead in your sins and the uncircumcision of your flesh, hath he quickened together with him, having forgiven you all trespasses."*

The Apostle Paul had the revelation. That is why he says that our citizenship has been restored and we now sit in heavenly places.

Eph 2v6 *"And hath raised us up together, and made us sit together in heavenly places in Christ Jesus."*

Eph 2v19 *"Now therefore ye are no more strangers and foreigners, but fellow citizens with the saints, and of the household of God."*
We must understand that we have entry to Heaven, but it is not our permanent residence. The revelation of the Scriptures is that earth is given to humanity as an eternal home and that it will remain forever.

Many preachers quote this Scripture in John, especially at funerals, that Jesus is still busy preparing the place for us. They are encouraging people to stay fast as their place has not been prepared yet. Just to hold on, struggle forth, He is coming.

Beloved, if Jesus Christ wanted you in heaven, you would have been there after His resurrection. He prays this important prayer.

John 17v3 *"And this is life eternal, that they might know thee the only true God, and Jesus Christ, whom thou hast sent."* **John 17v4** *"I have glorified thee on the earth: I have finished the work which thou gavest me to do. I have given them thy word; and the world hath hated them, because they are not of the world, even as I am not of the world."* **John 17v15** *"I pray not that thou shouldest take them out of the world, but that thou shouldest keep them from the evil."* **John 17v16** *"They are not of the world, even as I am not of the* *world.”* **John 17v17** *“Sanctify them through thy truth: thy word is truth.”*

Chapter 2: The Scriptures are revealed

The religious leaders could not understand the Spiritual Revelation.

John 3v5 *"Jesus answered, verily, verily, I say unto thee. Except a man be born of water and of the Spirit, he cannot enter into the kingdom of God."* **John 3v6** *"That which is born of the flesh is flesh; and that which is born of the Spirit, is spirit."* **John 3v7** *"Marvel not that I said unto thee, ye must be born again."*

The church is still somehow captured in the idea that some of us will be ruptured or plainly said; snatched from earth, when things get too difficult. We buy the one book after another as to why Jesus is returning; even the world hints about it and makes laws so we can give in and account to such laws.

Gal 5v1 *"Stand fast therefore in the liberty wherewith Christ hath made us free, and be not entangled again with the yoke of bondage."*

This speaks of Abba Father's freedom. Now, what is freedom? The definition of Biblical freedom is: Freedom is the ability to take voluntary decisions without coercion or the action or practice of persuading someone to do something by using force or threats. This means the table will be prepared and you choose what to eat; the whole Bible is about decisions, choices and the consequences thereof.

Where was God when Satan spoke to man? Remember that He is omniscient, almighty and omnipotent. So, He was there. Why didn't He intervene? The answer: freedom of choice. But even our freedom of choice is limited so that Abba Father, who is in us working in and through us.

Phil 2v13 *"For it is God which worked in you both to will and to do of his good pleasure."* **Phil 2v14** *"Do all things without murmurings and disputings:"* **Phil 2v15** *"That ye may be blameless and harmless, the sons of God, without rebuke, in the midst of a crooked and perverse nation, among whom ye shine as lights in the world."*

Chapter 3: The three places

Three places are identified in Abba Father's council.

Rom 11v33 *"O depth of the riches both of the wisdom and knowledge of God! How unsearchable are his judgments, and his ways past finding out!"* **Rom 11v34** *"For who hath known the mind of the Lord? Or who hath been his counsellor?"* **Rom 11v35** *"Or who hath first given to him and it shall be recompensed unto him again?"* **Rom 11v36** *"For of him, and through him, and to him, are all things: to whom be glory forever. Amen."*

So beloved, heaven and hell are physical places, like the earth.

Phil 2v9 *"Wherefore God also hath highly exalted him, and given him a name which is above every name."* **Phil 2v10** *"That at the name of Jesus every knee should bow, of things in heaven, and things in earth, and things under the earth."*

There are three places, and every place has residents or inhabitants. However, everything created belongs to the Lord.

Col 1v15 *"Who is the image of the invisible God, the firstborn of every creature."* **Col 1v16** *"For by him were all things created, that are in heaven, and that are in earth,* *visible and invisible, whether they be thrones, or dominions, or principalities, or powers: all things were created by him and for him."* **Col 1v17** *"And he is before all things, and by him all things consist."*

The question arises: How did people land on earth? The answer: Through the decision of the council of the Almighty Father.

Genesis 1v26 *"And God said, let us make man in our image, after our likeness; and let them have dominion over the fish of the sea, and over the fowl of the air, and over the cattle, and over all the earth, and over every creeping thing that crept upon the earth."* **Gen 1v27** *"So God created man in his own image, in the image of God created he him; male and female created he them."* **Gen 1v28** *"And God blessed them, and God said unto them be fruitful, and multiply and replenish the earth, and subdue it; and have dominion over the fish of the sea and over the fowl of the earth, and over every living thing that moved upon the earth."*

Psalm 100v3 *"Know yea that the Lord, he is God; it is he that made us, and not we ourselves; we are his people and the sheep of his pastures."*

Acts 17v26 *"And hath made of one blood all nations of men for to dwell on all the face of the earth and hath determined* *the times before appointed, and the bounds of their habitations."*

We see this; people are created by God and placed on earth with a purpose. Earth has been given to people to live in; not heaven or hell. People have become convinced that "this one is for us to decide."

Psalm 115v16 *"The heaven, even the heavens, are the LORD's; but the earth hath he given to the children of men."*

Matt 5v5 *"Blessed are the meek, for they shall inherit the earth."*

It is our responsibility as kings with Christ to seek after the plan of our Father.

Proverbs 25v2 *"It is the glory of God to conceal a thing; but the honour of kings is to search out a matter."*

Everyone is living a repenting life to make a difference in Heaven. You are created to make a difference today, child of the Highest. There should be a difference between those who serve Christ, and those who don't.

You are in the final time of faith as **Romans 5** describes: Your character is being formed to rule over your circumstances.

Rom 5v1 *"Therefore being justified by faith, we have peace with God through our Lord Jesus Christ."* **Rom 5v2** *"By whom also we have access by faith into this grace wherein we stand, and rejoice in hope of the glory of God."* **Rom 5v3** *"And not only so, but we glory in tribulations also: knowing that tribulation worked patience;"* **Rom 5v4** *"And patience, experience; and experience, hope."* **Rom 5v5** *"And hope maketh not ashamed; because the love of God is shed abroad in our hearts by the Holy Ghost which is given unto us."* **Rom 5v6** *"For when we were yet without strength, in due time Christ died for the ungodly."*

Adam was a living soul and could not do what we are able to do to move between heaven and earth. We will be life-giving spirits.

1 Cor 15v44 *"It is sown a natural body; it is raised a spiritual body. There is a natural body, and there is a spiritual body."* **1 Cor 15v45** *"And so it is written, the first man Adam was made a living soul; the last Adam was made a quickening spirit."*

The world today is confused because the god of this world is making people believe this is their eternal home. That there is no heavenly place, no hell, no God and no devil. The Scriptures teaches us that their ending is far from the glory of God.

Beloved, the righteousness will increase ... **Rom 5v14** *"Nevertheless death reigned from Adam to Moses, even over them that had not sinned after the similitude of Adam's transgression, who is the figure of him that was to come."* **Rom 5v15** *"But not as the offence, so also is the free gift. For if through the offence of one many be dead, much more the grace of God, and the gift by grace, which is by one man, Jesus Christ, hath abounded unto many."* **Rom 5v16** *"And not as it was by one that sinned, so is the gift: for the judgment was by one to condemnation, but the free gift is of many offences unto justification."* **Rom 5v17** *"For if by one man's offence death reigned by one; much more they which receive abundance of grace and of the gift of righteousness shall reign in life by one, Jesus Christ."* **Rom 5v18** *"Therefore as by the offence of one judgment came upon all men to condemnation; even so by the righteousness of one. the free gift came upon all men unto justification of life."* **Rom 5v19** *"For as by one man's disobedience many were made sinners, so by the obedience of one shall many be made righteous."* **Rom 5v20** *"Moreover the law entered, that the offence might abound. But where sin abounded, grace did much more abound:"*

We are here for a purpose, to be the instruments that the Father wants to use within this world. We must show His love and affection.

John 3v16 *"For God so loved the world, that he gave his only begotten Son, that whosoever believeth in him should not perish, but have eternal life."* **John 3v17** *"For God sent not his Son into the world to condemn the world; but that the world through him might be saved."*
We can only do this if we allow the Holy Spirit to pour out His love into our hearts.

Rom 5v5 *"And hope maketh not ashamed; because the love of God is shed abroad in our hearts by the Holy Ghost which is given unto us."*

Instead what do we do as the church? We have a "come to us" mentality and a "we go away from you" mindset.

Titus 2v11 *"For the grace of God that bringeth salvation hath appeared to all men."* **Titus 2v12** *"Teaching us that - denying ungodliness and worldly lusts, we should live soberly, righteously, and godly, in this present world."* **Titus 2v13** *"Looking for that blessed hope, and the glorious appearing of the great God and our Saviour Jesus Christ."* **Titus 2v14** *"Who gave himself for us, that he might redeem us from all iniquity, and purify unto himself a peculiar people, zealous of good works."*

When you have a Kingdom, mind set your light shines in a dark world, to give hope to those who perish and tell them about His coming and His grace. Beloved, if God is the owner of everything as said in **Psalm 24**, why take us away if we are the heirs, to give us something else? No beloved, He changed the system and made it Holy, removed the wicked and restored us in our righteous position.

The land which He promised to our forefathers, Abraham, Isaac and Jacob, that is the promise He must honour this as God cannot lie, He is watching to see His word fulfilled, for no matter how many promises God has made, they are *yes* in Christ.

Eph 1v13 *"In whom ye also trusted, after that ye heard the word of truth, the gospel of your salvation: in whom also after that ye believed, ye were sealed with that Holy Spirit of promise,"* **Eph 1v14** *"Which is the earnest of our inheritance until the redemption of the purchased possession, unto the praise of his glory."* **Eph 1v15** *"Wherefore I also, after I heard of your faith in the Lord Jesus, and love unto all the saints."* **Eph 1v16** *"Cease not to give thanks for you, making mention of you in my prayers."* **Eph 1v17** *"That the God of our Lord Jesus Christ, the Father of glory, may give unto you the spirit of wisdom and revelation in the knowledge of him."* **Eph 1v18** *"The eyes of your understanding being enlightened; that ye may know what is the hope of his calling, and what are the riches of the glory of his inheritance in the saints".* **Eph 1v19** *"And what is the exceeding greatness of his power to us-ward who believe, according to the working of his mighty power."* **Eph 1v20** *"Which he wrought in Christ, when he raised him from the dead, and set him at his* *own right hand in the heavenly places.* **Eph 1v21** *"Far above all principality, and power, and might, and dominion, and every name that is named, not only in this world, but also in that which is to come:"* **Eph 1v22** *"And hath put all things under his feet, and gave him to be the head over all things to the church,"* **Eph 1v23** *Which is his body, the fullness of him that filleth all in all."*

Wow, I am fully encouraged and overwhelmed with the knowledge that He who began a good work in me, will carry it on to completion until the day of Christ Jesus.

Phil 1v6 *"Being confident of this very thing, that he which hath begun a good work in you will perform it until the day of Jesus Christ."*

1 Cor 15v54 *"So when this corruptible shall have put on in corruption, and this mortal shall have put on immortality, then shall be brought to pass the saying that is written, Death is swallowed up in victory."* **1 Cor 15v55** *"O death, where is thy sting? O grave, where is thy victory?"* **1 Cor 15v56** *"The sting of death is sin; and the strength of sin is the law."* **1 Cor 15v57** *"But thanks be to God, which gives us the victory through our Lord Jesus Christ."* **1 Cor 15v58** *"Therefore, my beloved brethren, be ye steadfast, unmoveable, always abounding in the work of the Lord, for as much as ye know that your labour is not in vain in the Lord."*

Amazing that we have an overview as to what awaits us. Beloved, change your attitude towards this temporary world system as it will disappear like mist before the sun. Our work here is to influence this world with His Agape Love, to be the love thorn in the flesh, the Mordecai for the Haman's, a Noah for the ungodly people, a Moses for the Egyptians and a Jesus for the Pharisees, a Christ to the lost.

Rom 8v19 *"For the earnest expectation of the creature waiteth for the manifestation of the sons of God."* **Rom 8v20** *"For the creature was made subject to vanity, not willingly, but by reason of him who hath subjected the same in hope,"* **Rom 8v21** *"Because the creature itself also shall be delivered from the bondage of corruption into the glorious liberty of the children of God."* **Rom 8v22** *"For we know that the whole creation groaneth and travaileth in pain together until now."* **Rom 8v23** *"And not only they, but ourselves also, which have the first fruits of the Spirit, even we ourselves groan within ourselves, waiting for the adoption, to wit, the redemption of our body."*

Jesus told this story in **Luke 16** about a rich man, Lazarus and hell. No one has been saved until after the crucifixion and resurrection of Christ, Jesus said unto the evil doer: *"today you will live with me in paradise."* The Scriptures teaches us that He came down and then ascended into heaven.

Eph 4v9 *"Now that he ascended, what is it but that he also descended first into the lower parts of the earth?"* **Eph 4v10** *"He that descended is the same also that ascended up far above all heavens, that he might fill all things."*
Beloved, when the Lord said it is finished, He meant the restoration of our position in Him.

1 Cor 2v7 *"But we speak the wisdom of God in a mystery, even the hidden wisdom, which God ordained before the world unto our glory:"* **1 Cor 2v8** *"Which none of the princes of this world knew: for had they known it, they would not have crucified the Lord of glory."* **1 Cor 2v9** *"But as it is written, Eye hath not seen, nor ear heard, neither have entered into the heart of man, the things which God hath prepared for them that love him."* **1 Cor 2v10** *"But God hath revealed them unto us by his Spirit: for the Spirit searched all things, yea, and the deep things of God."*

When Satan realised this, he wanted Jesus to come down from the cross.

Luke 23v37 *"And saying, If thou be the king of the Jews, save thyself.*

You see Beloved, your citizenship has been restored at the crucifixion.

Phil 3v20 *"For our conversation is in heaven; from whence also we look for the Saviour, the Lord Jesus Christ."*

Eph 2v19 *"Now therefore ye are no more strangers and foreigners, but fellow citizens with the saints, and of the household of God,"* **Eph 2v20** *"And are built upon the foundation of the apostles and prophets, Jesus Christ himself being the chief cornerstone,"* **Eph 2v21** *"In whom all the building fitly framed together groweth unto an holy temple in the Lord."* **Eph 2v22** *"In whom ye also are built together for an habitation of God through the Spirit."*

We are restored in Christ so that **Genesis 1v26** can be fulfilled. We are already restored spiritually in the plan of Abba Father. If the decisions of the council have been changed, it is not in the scriptures and Satan would have won because he would have destroyed God's plan with His people. However, everything works together in the Father's perfect plan. Ask yourself this question: Why would Jesus come during the night to steal us away? There is no substance for the rapture or snitching, but there is substance for a reunion and change to be like Him when He arrives with the Holy ones.

The Scripture regarding the journey to heaven is not saying much, and just leaves me with more unanswered questions. Abba Father's original plan in **Ephesians 1** and **Genesis 1**, was to place people on earth to rule and live here. In **Genesis 3,** man is influenced to make a wrong decision.

Gen 3v15 *"And I will put enmity between thee and the woman, and between thy seed and her seed; it shall bruise thy head, and thou shalt bruise his heel".*

A promise is given and is being fulfilled.

Gal 4v4 *"But when the fullness of the time was come, God sent forth his Son, made of a woman, made under the law."*

Jesus came to fulfil the plan of the council.

1 John 3v8 *"He that committed sin is of the devil; for the devil sinned from the beginning. For this purpose, the Son of God was manifested, that he might destroy the works of the devil."*

So, the salvations plan of **Genesis 3v15** came into force, a plan where the angels desired to peer.

Heb 9v22 *"And almost all things are by the law purged with blood; and without shedding of blood is no remission."* **Heb 9v23** *"It was therefore necessary that the patterns of things in the heavens should be purified with these; but the heavenly things themselves with better sacrifices than these."* **Heb 9v24** *"For Christ is not entered into the holy places made* *with hands, which are the figures of the true; but into heaven itself, now to appear in the presence of God for us."*

1 Peter 1v12 *"Unto whom it was revealed, that not unto themselves, but unto us they did minister the things, which are now reported unto you by them that have preached the gospel unto you with the Holy Ghost sent down from heaven; which things the angels desire to look into."*
1 Cor 2v7 *"But we speak the wisdom of God in a mystery, even the hidden wisdom, which God ordained before the world unto our glory,"* **1 Cor 2v8** *"Which none of the princes of this world knew: for had they known it, they would not have crucified the Lord of glory."*

Satan, when he was still Lucifer, knew what was required to be in the presence of the Father's glory; holiness and grace. He knew without the perfect flow of blood, there is no salvation of sinners, because he once was a cherub.

Ezek 12v12 *"And the prince that is among them shall bear upon his shoulder in the twilight, and shall go forth: they shall dig through the wall to carry out thereby: he shall cover his face, that he see not the ground with his eyes."*
Ezek 12v13 *"My net also will I spread upon him, and he shall be taken in my snare: and I will bring him to Babylon to the land of the Chaldeans; yet shall he not see it, though he shall die there."* **Ezek 12v14** *"And I will scatter toward every wind all that are about him to help him, and all his*

bands; and I will draw out the sword after them. **Ezek 12v15** *"And they shall know that I am the LORD, when I shall scatter them among the nations, and disperse them in the countries."*

You see Beloved, Christ had to restore us here and keep us here.

John 17v15 *"I pray not that thou shouldest take them out of the world, but that thou shouldest keep them from the evil."* **John 17v16** *"They are not of the world, even as I am not of the world."* **John 17v17** *"Sanctify them through thy truth: thy word is truth."*

Rom 8v11 *"But if the Spirit of him that raised up Jesus from the dead dwell in you, he that raised up Christ from the dead shall also quicken your mortal bodies by his Spirit that dwelleth in you."*

Rom 8v14 *"For as many as are led by the Spirit of God, they are the sons of God."*

Rom 8v16 *"The Spirit itself beareth witness with our spirit, that we are the children of God."*

Rom 8v19 *"For the earnest expectation of the creature waiteth for the manifestation of the sons of God."* **Rom 8v20** *"For the creature was made subject to vanity, not willingly, but by reason of him who hath subjected the same in hope."*

Rom 8v21 *"Because the creature itself also shall be delivered from the bondage of corruption into the glorious liberty of the children of God."* **Rom 8v22** *"For we know that the whole creation groaneth and travaileth in pain together until now."* **Rom 8v23** *"And not only they, but ourselves also, which have the first fruits of the Spirit, even we ourselves groan within ourselves, waiting for the adoption, to wit, the redemption of our body."*

He promises Abraham, the father of faith, a city of which he would be the architect and the artist.

Heb 11v10 *"For he looked for a city which hath foundations, whose builder and maker is God."*

This scripture also teaches us that God cannot lie, and it is impossible for Him to lie, that's why He made a covenant with himself. Scripture is very clear that the Lord Jesus Christ is coming to earth. The question is then: Is man not going to heaven at all? No Beloved, that is not what is being said here, what is meant is that it will not be your eternal home. Man has access to heaven, at the resurrection graves were opened and about five hundred at a time left their graves to prove that there is life after physical death. Henog and Elijah was taken to heaven and this stands as a testimony for us.

The Apostle John was in the spirit when he saw where the rest of our brothers and sister were in Christ.

Rev 6v9 *"When he opened the fifth seal, I saw under the altar the souls of those who had been slain because of the word of God and the testimony they had maintained."* **Rev 6v10** *"They called out in a loud voice, 'How long, Sovereign Lord, holy and true, until you judge the inhabitants of the earth and avenge our blood?'"* **Rev 6v11** *"Then each of them was given a white robe, and they were told to wait a little longer, until the full number of their fellow servants, their brothers and sisters, were killed just as they had been."*

You see, you have access to heaven, but not before us. Paul speaks about the mystery to live outside the body is to be with Christ. **2 Cor 5v6-9** says we will live and reign with Christ for eternity. Something that is really striking is that after Jacob took the blessing from Esau, he experienced the revelation of that blessing. You see, until we have not come to the revelation of knowledge for what was entrusted unto us, we will never see it and take it into our possession.

Jacob fled and came to a place of rest in **Genesis 28v10-22** as well as **Genesis 35v15** Jacob's blessing got meaning and connected him with heaven. Isn't it strange that Jacob later became Israel? Isn't it strange that access was obtained between heaven and earth? Isn't it strange that Israel is the core of the Father's plan with earth? Isn't it strange that Jesus Christ was born in that area?

Let's look at a few scripts with promises.

2 Cor 13v1 *"This is the third time I am coming to you. In the mouth of two or three witnesses shall every word be established."*

Psalm 2v8 [Amp] *"Ask of Me, and I will assuredly give [You] the nations as Your inheritance, and the ends of the earth as Your possession."*

Psalm 115v15 *"Ye are blessed of the LORD which made heaven and earth."* **Psalm 115v16** *"The heaven, even the heavens, are the LORD'S: but the earth hath he given to the children of men."* **Psalm 115v17** *"The dead praise not the LORD, neither any that go down into silence."*

Psalm 21v9 *"Thou shalt make them as a fiery oven in the time of thine anger; the LORD shall swallow them up in his wrath, and the fire shall devour them."* **Psalm 21v10** *"Their fruit shalt thou destroy form the earth, and their seed from among the children of men."*

Psalm 25v13 *"His soul shall dwell at ease; and his seed shall inherit the earth."* **Psalm 25v14** *"The secret of the LORD is with them that fear him; and he will shew them his covenant."*

Psalm 37v18 *"The Lord knoweth the days of the upright; and their inheritance shall be forever."*

Psalm 37v28 *"For the LORD loveth judgment, and forsaketh not his saints; they are preserved forever, but the seed of the wicked shall be cut off."* **Psalm 37v29** *"The righteous shall inherit the land and dwell therein forever."*

Isaiah 60v21 *"Thy people also shall be all righteous; they shall inherit the land for ever, the branch of my planting, the work of my hands, that I may be glorified."*

Isaiah 13v9 *"Behold, the day of the LORD cometh, cruel both with wrath and fierce anger, to lay the land desolate: and he shall destroy the sinners thereof out of it."*

Matt 5v5 *"Blessed are the meek: for they shall inherit the earth."*
Rom 4v13 *"For the promise, that he should be the heir of the world, was not to Abraham, or to his seed, through the law, but through the righteousness of faith."*

2 Thess 2:8 *"And then shall that Wicked be revealed, whom the Lord shall consume with the spirit of his mouth, and shall destroy with the brightness of his coming:"*

In Noah's time, the ungodly were swept away in the flood.

Luke 17v25 *"But first must he suffer many things, and be rejected of this generation."* **Luke 17v26** *"And as it was in the days of Noe, so shall it be also in the days of the Son of man.* **Luke 17v27** *"They did eat, they drank, they married wives, they were given in marriage, until the day that Noe entered into the ark, and the flood came, and destroyed them all."* **Luke 17v28** *"Likewise also as it was in the days of Lot; they did eat, they drank, they bought, they sold, they planted, they builded.* **Luke 17v29** *"But the same day that Lot went out of Sodom it rained fire and brimstone from heaven, and destroyed them all."* **Luke 17v30** *"Even thus shall it be in the day when the Son of man is revealed."*

You see Beloved, the ungodly go where they choose to be; in a place that was meant for the devil and his fallen angels. Our

Father never made hell for man, men choose that place because they rejected the Grace of God.

Rev 22v12 *"And, behold, I come quickly; and my reward is with me, to give every man according as his work shall be."*

Beloved why would God come to earth with the New Jerusalem and all the holy ones to reward all here?

Rev. 1v7 *"You see he will come at a time and hour that no one expects. He will come like a thief in the night. In him there is no darkness, so it will be a bright day. His glory will make everyone sees him."*

1 Thess 4v16 *"For the Lord himself shall descend from heaven with a shout, with the voice of the archangel, and with the trump of God: and the dead in Christ shall rise first:"* **1 Thess 4v17** *"Then we which are alive and remain shall be caught up together with them in the clouds, to meet the Lord in the air: and so, shall we ever be with the Lord."* This is scripture that is misread

The word speaks about those of us who remain on earth, will be changed.

1 Cor 15v50 *"Now this I say, brethren that flesh and blood cannot inherit the kingdom of God; neither doth corruption inherit incorruption."* **1 Cor 15v51** *"Behold, I shew you a mystery; we shall not all sleep, but we shall all be changed".*

1 Cor 15v52 *"In a moment, in the twinkling of an eye, at the last trumpet: for the trumpet shall sound, and the dead shall be raised incorruptible, and we shall be changed."* **1 Cor 15v53** *"For this corruptible must put on incorruption, and this mortal must put on immortality."* **1 Cor 15v54** *"So when this corruptible shall have put on incorruption, and this mortal shall have put on immortality, then shall be brought to pass the saying that is written, Death is swallowed up in victory."* **1 Cor 15v55** *"O death, where is thy sting? O grave, where is thy victory?"*

We will be taken up in our glorified bodies and be like Him.

1 John 3v2 *"Beloved, now are we the sons of God, and it doth not yet appear what we shall be: but we know that, when he shall appear, we shall be like him; for we shall see him as he is."*
We will be moved with them and reunite with them, this means that the meeting will be in the air … the scripture does not say that we are going to heaven, no Beloved, then it will be D-day for this world.

Now you ask: But the earth will be totally ruined by fire and then a new heaven will come with a new earth? Beloved, God's word is like a consuming fire. What happened to the old you when you were re-born? The fire of the Word systematically erased the old you with the renewing of your mindset.

Rev 15v2 *"And I saw as it were a sea of glass mingled with fire: and them that had gotten the victory over the beast, and over his image, and over his mark, and over the number of his name, stand on the sea of glass, having the harps of God."*

The scripture reference takes me back to when I was a young Christian. I had a vision, but I couldn't understand it at all, and today I realise this is the vision I had. I see the souls of people below the earth and they scream but no-one can hear them. They look desperately to the roof which is made of glass, and they can see the glory of God and no-one hears them. Beloved, I want to go that far by saying that the ungodly will see the glory of the Holy Ones from the bottom part of the earth and they will be in pain forever whilst their choice of living away from the Grace of God. We (the saved) will remain on the earth and will unconsciously continue with a life in the presence of Christ.

A Believers faith does not get developed, they have many teachings but don't see the overcoming of their deeds. Do you know why? We are programmed by "if one day we will get into heaven." We do not live a life of discernment between the ungodly and the believers. Beloved, if earth was to be destroyed, the script in **Romans 8v19-22** is not applicable. We will be revealed as Children of Abba Father as the Father planned it from the beginning. It was promised to Abraham and David and a God that cannot lie will bring it into existence.

Heb 11v8 *"By faith Abraham, when he was called to go out into a place which he should after receive for an inheritance, obeyed; and he went out, not knowing whither he went."* **Heb 11v9** *"By faith he sojourned in the land of promise, as in a strange country, dwelling in tabernacles with Isaac and Jacob, the heirs with him of the same promise."* **Heb 11v10** *"For he looked for a city which hath foundations, whose builder and maker is God."*

John 17v4 *"I have glorified thee on the earth: I have finished the work which thou gavest me to do.*

John 19v30 *"When Jesus therefore had received the vinegar, he said, It is finished: and he bowed his head, and gave up the ghost."*

He has united the heart of man with that of the Father. He was the mediator.

1 Tim 2v5 *"For there is one God, and one mediator between God and men, the man Christ Jesus."*

Gal 3v19 *"Wherefore then serveth the law? It was added because of transgressions, till the seed should come to whom the promise was made; and it was ordained by angels in the hand of a mediator."*

His blood cleansed and sanctified us from all iniquities for those who believe in Him.

Matt 6v33 *"But seek ye first the Kingdom of God and His righteousness."*
He has purified us, He sanctified us.

Rom 8v30 *"Moreover whom he did predestinate, them he also called: and whom he called, them he also justified: and whom he justified, them he also glorified."* **Rom 8v31** *"What shall we then say to these things? If God be for us, who can be against us?* **Rom 8v32** *"He that spared not his own Son, but delivered him up for us all, how shall he not with him also freely give us all things?"* **Rom 8v33** *"Who shall lay anything to the charge of God's elect? It is God that justifieth."* **Rom 8v34** *"Who is he that condemneth? It is Christ that died, yea rather, that is risen again, who is even at the right hand of God, who also maketh intercession for us."* **Rom 8v35** *"Who shall separate us from the love of Christ? shall tribulation, or distress, or persecution, or famine, or nakedness, or peril, or sword?"* **Rom 8v36** *"As it is written, For thy sake we are killed all the day long; we are accounted as sheep for the slaughter."* **Rom 8v37** *"Nay, in all these things we are more than conquerors through him that loved us."*

Christ finished the plan and assured our place in Him, we are sealed.

Eph 1v13 *"In whom ye also trusted, after that ye heard the word of truth, the gospel of your salvation: in whom also after that ye believed, ye were sealed with that holy Spirit of promise."*

Eph 4v30 *"And grieve not the holy Spirit of God, whereby ye are sealed unto the day of redemption."*
We have the Holy Spirit in us, who Christ revealed unto us so that the old self can die to do the work of the Father.

Eph 2v10 *"For we are his workmanship, created in Christ Jesus unto good works, which God hath before ordained that we should walk in them."*

The problem is that we don't do the work of winning of souls, bearing the Good News. Jesus prays in **John 17v9-16** – He answers the finishing of His task that we are not from this world.

John 17v9 *"I pray for them: I pray not for the world, but for them which thou hast given me; for they are thine."* **John 17v10** *"And all mine are thine, and thine are mine; and I am glorified in them."* **John 17v11** *"And now I am no more in the world, but these are in the world, and I come to thee. Holy Father, keep through thine own name those whom thou hast given me, that they may be one, as we are."* **John 17v12** *"While I was with them in the world, I kept them in thy name: those that thou gavest me I have kept, and none of them is lost, but the son of perdition; that the scripture might be* *fulfilled."* **John 17v13** *"And now come I to thee; and these things I speak in the world, that they might have my joy fulfilled in themselves."* **John 17v14** *"I have given them thy word; and the world hath hated them, because they are not of the world, even as I am not of the world."* **John 17v15** *"I pray not that thou shouldest take them out of the world, but that thou shouldest keep them from the evil."* **John 17v16** *"They are not of the world, even as I am not of the world."*

We are now in the spiritual realm of the righteous life. Daily we must be led by the Spirit, we must lay off the old self and put on the new man in Christ Jesus.

1 Cor 15v44 *"It is sown a natural body; it is raised a spiritual body. There is a natural body, and there is a spiritual body."* **1 Cor 15v45** *"And so it is written, the first man Adam was made a living soul; the last Adam was made a quickening spirit."* **1 Cor 15v46** *"Howbeit that was not first which is spiritual, but that which is natural; and afterward that which is spiritual."* **1 Cor 15v47** *"The first man is of the earth, earthy; the second man is the Lord from heaven."* **1 Cor 15v48** *"As is the earthy; such are they also that are earthy: and as is the heavenly, such are they also that are heavenly."* **1 Cor 15v49** *"And as we have borne the image of the earthy, we shall also bear the image of the heavenly."*

Scripture teaches us that Adam was a living soul and the Bible teaches us that God visited him in the Garden of Eden and he had no access to heaven. When God threw them out of the Garden of Eden, angels with swords of fire guarded the path.

Gen 3v23 *"Therefore the LORD God sent him forth from the Garden of Eden, to till the ground from whence he was taken."* **Gen 3v24** *"So he drove out man; and he placed at the east of the garden of Eden cherubims, and a flaming sword which turned every way, to keep the way of the tree of life."*

Let us stand still on this one: cherubs. They were assigned to guard the Garden of Eden, not normal angels, so what makes them so special? The tree of life was still left, and if man were to eat of that tree, the salvation's plan would be terminated. The cherub is a heavenly creature who protects the glory, the holiness and the grace of Abba Father.

Ex 25v18 *"And thou shalt make two cherubims of gold, of beaten work shalt thou make them, in the two ends of the mercy seat."* **Ex 25v19** *"And make one cherub on the one end, and the other cherub on the other end: even of the mercy seat shall ye make the cherubims on the two ends thereof."* **Ex 25v20** *"And the cherubims shall stretch forth their wings on high, covering the mercy seat with their wings, and their faces shall look one to another; toward the mercy seat shall the faces of the cherubims be."* **Ex 25v21** *"And thou shalt* *put the mercy seat above upon the ark; and in the ark, thou shalt put the testimony that I shall give thee."* **Ex 25v22** *"And there I will meet with thee, and I will commune with thee from above the mercy seat, from between the two cherubims which are upon the ark of the testimony, of all things which I will give thee in commandment unto the children of Israel."*

What I'm reading is that he was not banned from heaven; reason being: because he was not made to live in heaven.

Gen 1v26 *"And God said, Let us make man in our image, after our likeness: and let them have dominion over the fish of the sea, and over the fowl of the air, and over the cattle, and over all the earth, and over every creeping thing that creepeth upon the earth."* **Gen 1v27** *"So God created man in his own image, in the image of God created he him; male and female created he them."* **Gen 1v28** *"And God blessed them, and God said unto them, be fruitful, and multiply, and replenish the earth, and subdue it: and have dominion over the fish of the sea, and over the fowl of the air, and over every living thing that moveth upon the earth."*

Chapter 4: After Jesus took the Disciples to the Mountain of Glory

Matt 17v1 *"And after six days Jesus taketh Peter, James and John his brother, and bringeth them up into a high mountain apart."* **Matt 17v2** *"And was transfigured before them: and his face did shine as the sun, and his raiment was white as the light."* **Matt 17v3** *"And behold, there appeared unto them Moses and Elias talking with him."*

He gave them a foretaste of what awaits them on His return to earth. Moses and Elias's lives and their bodies are glorified within Christ. After the Lord has reconciled man with Abba Father through the crucifixion.

Eph 2v13 *"But now in Christ Jesus you who once were far away have been brought near by the blood of Christ."* **Eph 2v14** *"For he himself is our peace, who has made the two groups one and has destroyed the barrier, the dividing wall of hostility."* **Eph 2v15** *"By setting aside in his flesh the law with its commands and regulations, His purpose was to create in himself one new humanity out of the two, thus making peace."* **Eph 2v16** *"And in one body to reconcile both of them to God through the cross, by which he put to death in hostility."* **Eph 2v17** *"He came and preached peace to you who were far away and peace to those who were near."* **Eph 2v18** *"For through him we both have access to the Father by one Spirit."*

The wonderful thing about it all is, after His ascension there was peace. The angels were left behind as witnesses, the cherubims Beloved, but this time without swords, to give us Hope and not to keep us out but to get us back through the tree of life; Christ.

Acts 1v8 *"But you will receive power when the Holy Spirit comes on you; and you will be my witnesses in Jerusalem, and all in Judea and Samaria, and to the ends of the earth."* **Acts 1v9** *"After he said this, he was taken up before their very eyes, and a cloud hid him from their sight."* **Acts 1v10** *"They were looking intently up into the sky as he was going, when suddenly two men dressed in white stood beside them."* **Acts 1v11** *"Men of Galilee,"* they said, *"why do you stand here looking into the sky? This same Jesus, who has been taken from you into heaven, will come back in the same way you have seen him into heaven."*

Think about this Beloved.

Phil 2v6 *"Who, being in the form of God, thought it not robbery to be equal with God."* **Phil 2v7** *"But made himself of no reputation, and took upon him the form of a servant, and was made in the likeness of men."* **Phil 2v8** *"And being found in fashion as a man, he humbled himself, and became obedient unto death, even the death of the cross."*

The price that our Lord had to pay is very deep and humiliating in the sense that He who did not know sin, became sin, He that did not know ungodliness, took on ungodliness. Just think about it for a moment: Jesus needed to take on the form of man, who would eventually age, who was not glorified; a body that needed food, that got tired, that needed to be cleansed, that needed to use the toilet. Beloved He did this all for us. Your salvation did not come cheap. Our Father did not restore us in heaven; He restored us on earth, why would He take us away from here?

Chapter 5: The separation

Beloved every eye shall experience that day. Look up for the King of kings will appear in the heavens. Read the Scriptures for yourself.

Matt 24v27 *"For as the lightning cometh out of the east, and shineth even unto the west; so, shall also the coming of the Son of man be."* **Matt 24v28** *"For wheresoever the carcase is, there will the eagles be gathered together."* **Matt 24v29** *"Immediately after the tribulation of those days shall the sun be darkened, and the moon shall not give her light, and the stars shall fall from heaven, and the powers of the heavens shall be shaken:"* **Matt 24v30** *"And then shall appear the sign of the Son of man in heaven: and then shall all the tribes of the earth mourn, and they shall see the Son of man coming in the clouds of heaven with power and great glory."* **Matt 24v31** *"And he shall send his angels with a great sound of a trumpet, and they shall gather together his elect from the four winds, from one end of heaven to the other."*

Beloved the Godly and the ungodly will stand together they will see us in our glorious bodies and move from the earth up into the heavens to be united with the Lord.

Matt 25v31 *"When the Son of man shall come in his glory, and all the holy angels with him, then shall he sit upon the throne of his glory."* **Matt 25v32** *"And before him shall be* *gathered all nations: and he shall separate them one from another, as a shepherd divideth his sheep from the goats."* **Matt 25v33** *"And he shall set the sheep on his right hand, but the goats on the left.* **Matt 25v34** *"Then shall the King say unto them on his right hand, Come, ye blessed of my Father, inherit the kingdom prepared for you from the foundation of the world."*

So, when the trumpet shall sound, the separation will take place. Beloved, you must have the deposit, the mark of the Holy Spirit inside and on you. Those that will dwell with Him in His Heavenly Kingdom will be the sheep; the goats will look up to the heavens from the earth. Many believe in Him, but do not accept Him. All who believe in Him and accept Him, unto them has been given the power to be called children of God.

John 1v12 *"But as many as received him, to them gave he power to become the sons of God, even to them that believe on his name."*

Just something to think about. What did the Christ show to the Apostles? Jesus started His preaching in Matthew 5.

Matt 5v14 *"Ye are the light of the world. A city that is set on an hill cannot be hid."*

He goes on further and leads the disciples to the top of the mountain. What did He want them to see?

Matt 17v1 *"And after six days Jesus taketh Peter, James, and John his brother, and bringeth them up into an high mountain apart,"* **Matt 17v2** *"And was transfigured before them: and his face did shine as the sun, and his raiment was white as the light."* **Matt 17v3** *"And, behold, there appeared unto them Moses and Elias talking with him."* **Matt 17v4** *"Then answered Peter, and said unto Jesus, 'Lord, it is good for us to be here: if thou wilt, let us make here three tabernacles; one for thee, and one for Moses, and one for Elias'."*

Did you notice that they haven't concluded fully understanding the revelation and wanted to build a city immediately, a physical city?

Beloved, God is Spirit and wants to be worshipped in Spirit and in Truth. Don't look for a physical city. Abraham looked forward to the City built by God Himself.

When you read through the Scriptures below, you will notice in the Spirit, that the City is not a physical place as it is known to people, but a dwelling place of God's Spirit.

Revelation speaks about the City as the Bride of Christ, as revealed to Saint John at Patmos while he was in the Spirit.

Rev 3v12 *"Him that overcometh will I make a pillar in the temple of my God, and he shall go no more out: and I will* *write upon him the name of my God, and the name of the city of my God, which is new Jerusalem, which cometh down out of heaven from my God: and I will write upon him my new name.*

Rev 21v22 *"And I saw no temple therein: for the Lord God Almighty and the Lamb are the temple of it."* **Rev 21v23** *"And the city had no need of the sun, neither of the moon, to shine in it: for the glory of God did lighten it, and the Lamb is the light thereof."* **Rev 21v24** *"And the nations of them which are saved shall walk in the light of it: and the kings of the earth do bring their glory and honour into it."* **Rev 21v25** *"And the gates of it shall not be shut at all by day: for there shall be no night there."* **Rev 21v26** *"And they shall bring the glory and honour of the nations into it."* **Rev 21v27** *"And there shall in no wise enter into it anything that defileth, neither whatsoever worketh abomination, or maketh a lie: but they which are written in the Lamb's book of life."*

1 Chr 15v1 *"And David made him houses in the city of David, and prepared a place for the ark of God, and pitched for it a tent."* **1 Chr 15v2** *"Then David said, None ought to carry the ark of God but the Levites: for them hath the LORD chosen to carry the ark of God, and to minister unto him for ever."*

Acts 4v11 *"This is the stone which was set at nought of you builders, which is become the head of the corner."*

Acts 17v22 *"Then Paul stood in the midst of Mars' hill, and said, Ye men of Athens, I perceive that in all things ye are too superstitious."* **Acts 17v23** *"For as I passed by, and beheld your devotions, I found an altar with this inscription, TO THE UNKNOWN GOD. Whom therefore ye ignorantly worship, him declare I unto you."* **Acts 17v24** *"God that made the world and all things therein, seeing that he is Lord of heaven and earth, dwelleth not in temples made with hands."* **Acts 17v25** *"Neither is worshipped with men's hands, as though he needed anything, seeing he giveth to all life, and breath, and all things."* **Acts 17v26** *"And hath made of one blood all nations of men for to dwell on all the face of the earth, and hath determined the times before appointed, and the bounds of their habitation."* **Acts 17v27** *"That they should seek the Lord, if haply they might feel after him, and find him, though he be not far from every one of us."* **Acts 17v28** *"For in him we live, and move, and have our being; as certain also of your own poets have said, For we are also his offspring."* **Acts 17v29** *"For as much then as we are the offspring of God, we ought not to think that the Godhead is like unto gold, or silver, or stone, graven by art and man's device."*

1 Cor 3v9 *"For we are labourers together with God: ye are God's husbandry, ye are God's building."* **1 Cor 3v10** *"According to the grace of God which is given unto me, as a wise master builder, I have laid the foundation, and another buildeth thereon. But let every man take heed how he* *buildeth thereupon."* **1 Cor 3v11** *"For other foundation can no man lay than that is laid, which is Jesus Christ."* **1 Cor 3v12** *"Now if any man build upon this foundation gold, silver, precious stones, wood, hay, stubble."* **1 Cor 3v13** *"Every man's work shall be made manifest: for the day shall declare it, because it shall be revealed by fire; and the fire shall try every man's work of what sort it is."* **1 Cor 3v14** *"If any man's work abide which he hath built thereupon, he shall receive a reward."* **1 Cor 3v15** *"If any man's work shall be burned, he shall suffer loss: but he himself shall be saved; yet so as by fire."* **1 Cor 3v16** *"Know ye not that ye are the temple of God, and that the Spirit of God dwelleth in you?"* **1 Cor 3v17** *"If any man defile the temple of God, him shall God destroy; for the temple of God is holy, which temple ye are."* **1 Cor 3v18** *"Let no man deceive himself. If any man among you seemeth to be wise in this world, let him become a fool, that he may be wise."* **1 Cor 3v19** *"For the wisdom of this world is foolishness with God. For it is written, He taketh the wise in their own craftiness."* **1 Cor 3v20** *"And again, The Lord knoweth the thoughts of the wise, that they are vain."*

Eph 2v19 *"Now therefore ye are no more strangers and foreigners, but fellow citizens with the saints, and of the household of God."* **Eph 2v20** *"And are built upon the foundation of the apostles and prophets, Jesus Christ himself being the chief corner stone."* **Eph 2v21** *"In whom all the building fitly framed together groweth unto an holy temple in* *the Lord"* **Eph 2v22** *"In whom ye also are builded together for an habitation of God through the Spirit."*

1 Peter 2v6 *"Wherefore also it is contained in the scripture, Behold, I lay in Sion a chief corner stone, elect, precious: and he that believeth on him shall not be confounded."* **1 Peter 2v7** *"Unto you therefore which believe he is precious: but unto them which be disobedient, the stone which the builders disallowed, the same is made the head of the corner."* **1 Peter 2v8** *"And a stone of stumbling, and a rock of offence, even to them which stumble at the word, being disobedient: whereunto also they were appointed."* **1 Peter 2v9** *"But ye are a chosen generation, a royal priesthood, an holy nation, a peculiar people; that ye should shew forth the praises of him who hath called you out of darkness into his marvellous light."*

Rev 1v1 *"The Revelation of Jesus Christ, which God gave unto him, to shew unto his servants things which must shortly come to pass; and he sent and signified it by his angel unto his servant John."* **Rev 1v2** *"Who bare record of the word of God, and of the testimony of Jesus Christ, and of all things that he saw."* **Rev 1v3** *"Blessed is he that readeth, and they that hear the words of this prophecy, and keep those things which are written therein: for the time is at hand."* **Rev 1v4** *"John to the seven churches which are in Asia: Grace be unto you, and peace, from him which is, and which was, and which is to come; and from the seven Spirits which are before his throne."*

Rev 1v10 *"I was in the Spirit on the Lord's day, and heard behind me a great voice, as of a trumpet."* **Rev 1v11** *"Saying, I am Alpha and Omega, the first and the last: and, What thou seest, write in a book, and send it unto the seven churches which are in Asia; unto Ephesus, and unto Smyrna, and unto Pergamos, and unto Thyatira, and unto Sardis, and unto Philadelphia, and unto Laodicea."* **Rev 1v12** *"And I turned to see the voice that spake with me. And being turned, I saw seven golden candlesticks."* **Rev 1v13** *"And in the midst of the seven candlesticks one like unto the Son of man, clothed with a garment down to the foot, and girt about the paps with a golden girdle."*

Rev 1v20 *"The mystery of the seven stars which thou sawest in my right hand, and the seven golden candlesticks. The seven stars are the angels of the seven churches: and the seven candlesticks which thou sawest are the seven churches."*

1 Cor 2v7 *But we speak the wisdom of God in a mystery, even the hidden wisdom, which God ordained before the world unto our glory."* **1 Cor 2v8** *"Which none of the princes of this world knew: for had they known it, they would not have crucified the Lord of glory."* **1 Cor 2v9** *"But as it is written, Eye hath not seen, nor ear heard, neither have entered into the heart of man, the things which God hath prepared for them that love him."* **1 Cor 2v10** *"But God hath revealed them unto us by his Spirit: for the Spirit searcheth* *all things, yea, the deep things of God."* **1 Cor 2v11** *"For what man knoweth the things of a man, save the spirit of man which is in him? even so the things of God knoweth no man, but the Spirit of God."* **1 Cor 2v12** *Now we have received, not the spirit of the world, but the spirit which is of God; that we might know the things that are freely given to us of God."*

This will be a sad day for those who rejected Christ they will go to a place that was never indented for them.

Matt 25v41 *"Then shall he say also unto them on the left hand, Depart from me, ye cursed, into everlasting fire, prepared for the devil and his angels."*

If you believe in the rapture or not has nothing to do with your salvation in Christ. If you believe with your heart and confess Him Lord of your life that He died for your sins; rose on the third day, was taken up in heaven and sets you free. You are born again. Is your life right with Christ? Do you not just know about Him? Do you know Him as your personal Saviour?

If your answer is no, invite Him into your life. Pray: *"Lord Jesus, thank You that You have died for me on the cross of Calvary. I repent of my sins before You and make You King and Lord of my life. Fill me with Your Holy Spirit and teach me about our Heavenly Father ... AMEN."*

I experienced the favour of God and His goodness.

Psalm 5v12 *"For thou, LORD, wilt bless the righteous; with favour wilt thou compass him as a shield."*

Psalm 35v27 *"Let them shout for joy and be glad, that favour my righteous cause: yea, let them say continually, let the LORD be magnified, which hath pleasure in the prosperity of his servant."*
When you serve the Lord with love, His Spirit pours out into your heart, and it casts out every fear.

Rom 5v5 *"And hope maketh not ashamed; because the love of God is shed abroad in our hearts by the Holy Ghost which is given unto us."*

John 3v3 *"Jesus answered and said unto him, Verily, verily, I say unto thee, Except a man be born again, he cannot see the Kingdom of God."* **John 3v4** *"Nicodemus saith unto him, How can a man be born when he is old? can he enter the second time into his mother's womb, and be born?"* **John 3v5** *"Jesus answered, Verily, verily, I say unto thee, Except a man be born of water and of the Spirit, he cannot enter into the Kingdom of God."*

Abba Father loves you, he already dealt with your sins you just must believe and accept Him in your heart.

Rom 5v8 *"But God commendeth his love toward us, in that, while we were yet sinners, Christ died for us."* **Rom 5v9** *"Much more then, being now justified by his blood, we shall be saved from wrath through him."*

To be part of His Family you need to become a Son?

John 1v12 *"But as many as received him, to them gave he power to become the sons of God, even to them that believe on his name."*

Keep the Faith.

To be continued ... "What is heaven like."